Olde Missus Milliwhistle's

book of

Beneficial Beasties

Enjoy!

R.P. Lil

Val and Ron Lindahn

VAL LINDAHN

LONGSTREET PRESS, INC.
Atlanta, Georgia

Published by
LONGSTREET PRESS, INC.
A subsidiary of Cox Newspapers,
A subsidiary of Cox Enterprises, Inc.
2140 Newmarket Parkway
Suite 122
Marietta, GA 30067

Printed in the United States of America

1st printing 1997

Library of Congress Catalog Card Number: 96-79796

ISBN 1-56352-395-7

Book design by Graham and Company Graphics
Jacket design by Neil Hollingsworth
Separations and Imaged by OGI, Forest Park, GA

Dedication

For Julia Mather and Rose-Mary Hatfield

Val Lindahn, October 1996

For Chuck Perry, John Yow and the team at
Longstreet Press for having faith in our work and for
their assistance in bringing our dreams into reality.

Ron Lindahn, October 1996

Once upon a time, not long ago, in a land called Rabun, there was a mountain named for part of a famous army general. The general's name was Pickens, and the part was his nose.

Olde Missus Milliwhistle was sitting on Pickens Nose (not the General but the mountain) reading a book. As she read, she started talking to herself, muttering and sputtering, fussing and fuming. She made such a racket that her friends in the forest came to see what had upset her so.

The first to arrive was Elizabeth Lizard, who ran right up onto Missus Milliwhistle's big book and asked her what was the matter. Before she could answer, Buford Beetle crawled out from beneath a big red and yellow leaf. He stretched his little wings out wide, yawned, and asked what all the commotion was about. Then he fluttered up next to Liz atop Missus Milliwhistle's book.

Missus Milliwhistle started to explain when they all heard a rustling sound nearby. Then came a loud croak. It was their friend, Frog, who was formerly known as Prince. He bounced his way over to them and he appeared to be hopping mad.

Buford Beetle looked at Frog and saw that his bottom lip was sticking out, all pouty like. Of course this made Frog look rather silly, and Buford would have laughed, but that might have upset Frog even more.

"What's the matter?" asked Buford.

"You are having a story time and I wasn't invited" said Frog.

"Silly Frog," said Liz. "We just came to see what was wrong with Missus Milliwhistle."

Once Frog had joined the others atop her book, Missus Milliwhistle explained that she had just been reading to herself. It was not story time.

"Why are you so upset?" Buford asked.

"Oh, it's this book. They have most of the stories all wrong," Missus Milliwhistle replied.

"What are the stories about?" asked Liz.

"They're all about mythological creatures."

"Miffed illogical creatures?" croaked Frog. He had not been paying proper attention to the conversation because he was still pouting.

"No, mythological creatures. Those are creatures that don't really exist. Someone just made them up out of their head," said Buford Beetle, very proud to know the correct answer because he had been paying close attention.

"And that is just the problem," Missus Milliwhistle replied. "In the first place, most of them do exist, or at least they did once upon a time. In the second place, these stories make some of the creatures sound evil and nasty and no fun at all. And in the third place, they talk about these creatures doing the things they do for all the wrong reasons."

"But if it's written down in the book, it must be true," said Frog, *paying very close attention now.*

"No," Missus Milliwhistle said. "Just because it's in a book doesn't make it true."

"Why would they write the stories wrong?" Liz asked.

"I believe it's because these stories were written by grumpy old men who didn't like their jobs," Missus Milliwhistle replied. "They didn't like their jobs, so they took their frustration out on everyone else.

"Why, I used to know one grumpy old man who thought that the little forest fairies were pests. He made himself a big fairy-swatter, and he would sit out on his front porch all afternoon yelling, 'Come on, you pesky little flying varmints.' Fortunately, he was slow and the fairies were very quick. Just the same, he kept threatening to use them to spice his waffles. He never realized that it was the fairies who put the dew drops on the grass early in the morning. Even worse, his friend, Lady Cottington, used to catch fairies and keep them pressed between the pages of a book. You see, they simply missed the point."

"And what is the point?" asked Buford.

"The point is that the world really is full of magic and wonder. Every person and every creature is here for a purpose, and that purpose always has some benefit to everything else."

"So how are we ever to know what is true?" asked Buford.

"Oh, I know that one!" Liz exclaimed. "You have to think for yourself."

"Exactly," said Missus Milliwhistle. "I have even made up rhymes to help me remember what I think about my favorite mythological creatures. I call them my little beasties. Would you like to hear about them?" she asked.

"Oh, yes!" replied Liz and Buford in a chorus.

"See, I knew it was a story time," muttered Frog under his breath.

So Olde Missus Milliwhistle began to tell her friends about her favorite creatures.

Missus Milliwhistle pointed to the page she had been reading from and said, "A good example of how things are not always what they seem to be is the story of the troll. It says here that trolls are nasty, hateful beasts who roam the countryside picking fights with everyone and everything.

"You see, trolls are very big and not too pretty to look at. They don't like to comb their hair or wear new clothes, and they are a bit clumsy. It is just because of their looks that writers always make them the villains in their stories. In fact, most trolls are very gentle and kind.

"For instance, the story about the troll who lived under the bridge says that he would jump out and grab unsuspecting goats that tried to cross. The truth is that every time the poor troll tried to lie down for a nap the mischievous goats would stomp across the wooden bridge, making as much noise as they could, just to wake him up."

The Troll

Alas the Troll all gnarled and bent,
beneath a bridge his life's been spent.
Harassed by goats, both young and old,
and still his story's ne'er been told.
You see, he's really not that bad;
he's just depressed and feeling sad.
Now lying there in hidden heap,
he only wants to get some sleep.

"Now as for gorgons," Missus Milliwhistle continued, turning the page, "they were supposed to be fearsome winged beasts with snakes for hair. It was said that anyone who looked at them would instantly turn to stone. Once again this story is all wrong. It was probably written by a grumpy old man who was jealous of Medusa's power.

"The famous Medusa, for example, was actually a gorgon who granted immortality to creatures who wished to bring joy and happiness to others. If they asked her, she would transform them into small figurines that could sit still forever on a shelf or mantle. This way they could watch over the people who loved them and brought them home. The little creatures are sometimes called knickknacks because they have a 'knack' for sending out helpful thoughts just in the 'knick' of time."

The Gorgon

The Gorgon with her stony stare
and writhing wriggling mass of hair,
transforms the creatures great and small
we find for sale down at the mall —
the porcelain kitties, ducks, and dogs,
marble penguins, granite hogs.
I love my shelves of tiny friends
and hope her power never ends.

Buford said, "My mother told me I had a cousin named Scarab who lives very far away. She said that he used to know a giant creature called a stinks."

"I think you mean a sphinx," Missus Milliwhistle replied with a smile. "The sphinx was supposed to be a great beast with the body of a lion and the head of a woman or man. In most stories the sphinx would lie in wait along the road to a city or temple. When a person tried to pass, the sphinx would ask a riddle. If the person didn't know the answer, then the sphinx would devour him.

"This is complete nonsense. You see, sphinxes are made mostly of stone, which makes them move very slowly. They also think slowly and have trouble making up their minds. Whenever someone happens by, the sphinx asks questions simply to learn what that person thinks. As a result, sphinxes have a hard time making decisions because they pay more attention to other people's thoughts than they pay to their own."

The Sphinx

If you observed the mighty Sphinx,
you'd be surprised at what she thinks —
of hot fudge sundaes and banana splits,
bright red cherries without the pits,
of chocolate cookies with chocolate chips,
and soda oceans with candy ships.
For eons resting there inert
she's tried to choose the best dessert.

"And here we have the griffin," said Missus Milliwhistle, turning another page. "Griffins, with the body of a lion and head and wings of a bird, were called the hounds of Zeus. They were supposed to be fierce guardians of treasure and gold. It is even reported that they made their homes in nests high atop cliffs and laid jewels instead of eggs.

"I think this is just wishful thinking on the part of a grumpy old man who thought he might track down such a creature and steal its treasure in order to get rich quick. The griffin is actually much smaller than a lion, lives in the forest, and is quite playful. They remind me of flying kittens. I have never known a griffin who cared at all for treasure or gold. They are quite content to enjoy the out-of-doors and play with other creatures."

The Griffin

The Griffin in his tabby way
dreams of flying mice at play.
He'll swat them as they flutter by,
or pounce from clouds in crystal sky,
then perch atop a catnip tree,
commanding all that he can see.
He'll wake up, when sleep is through,
to find his dreams have all come true.

"In the ocean there are lovely creatures known as sirens," Missus Milliwhistle went on. "Sirens are also called mermaids. In some old stories sirens were said to sing beautiful songs that would lure sailors to crash their ships on the rocks and drown. There are even stories of sailors who plugged their ears with beeswax so that they wouldn't be tempted by the beautiful music of the sirens.

"Can you believe it? The truth is that sirens helped seafaring men; they never hurt them. Any sailor lucky enough to land on an island inhabited by sirens enjoyed not only heavenly music but deliciously prepared seafood, fresh from the ocean, followed by a night of deep, restful sleep. It is pretty clear to me that these stories come from men who have never really seen a siren or mermaid. Come to think of it, that's probably why they are grumpy."

The Siren

The Siren's song so sweet and clear
all good sailors long to hear.
Most agree it's for her looks,
but those who know she also cooks
understand her plaintiff song
only means that dinner's on.
To dine with her they'd swim the sea
and eat their fill and sleep 'til three.

"Excuse me," Liz said. "Once I saw a picture of a beautiful flying lizard. I showed my mother the picture and asked if I could have wings when I grow up. She told me that it was a picture of a dragon and that dragons don't really exist."

"Don't be silly," Missus Milliwhistle said. "Dragons are some of my favorite beasties. I keep hearing that dragons don't really exist. Bah! I once read a book where a little girl named Melissa raised dragons as pets. *How to Choose Your Dragon* — it was a wonderful book. After reading it I went right down to the pet shop and got my own pet dragon. It's a cute little Dweeb called Gorp.

"So don't let anyone tell you that dragons aren't real. There are many different kinds of dragons, and they come in many shapes and sizes. And dragons are not at all fearsome. They are friendly and fun to play with."

The Dragon

Behold the Dragon strong and fair
with treasure hoarded in his lair.
'Tis the dream of every child
to tame a dragon from the wild
and fly with him on leathery wings
to visit princes, knights, and kings.
The dragon's strength and magic charm
will keep all children safe from harm.

"And Liz, here's another creature they say doesn't really exist," Missus Milliwhistle said, pointing to the next picture.

"I know how much you like horses, so you will probably like centaurs as well. Part human, part horse, the stories say that centaurs were uncouth and savage. The same stories also say that some centaurs, like Chiron, were the teachers of men. If both stories were true, it might explain why some men are uncouth and savage.

"Actually centaurs live a very peaceful, balanced life. They work hard but always make time to romp and play every day. They also enjoy learning and are fond of reading. In the old days a person who lived a balanced life was said to be 'centaured.' When a person started acting a little crazy or spent too much time doing just one thing, like watching television, they were said to be 'off-centaur.' The words have changed over time and now we call such a person off-center."

The Centaur

The Centaur, neither beast nor man,
rides herself, fast as she can.
She dances jigs, she trots and prances,
she kicks her hooves with sideways glances.
And when she's finished with her run,
she turns to other things for fun.
Nestled down in leafy nook,
she finds great pleasure in a book.

The Secret Lives of Cats

LONG STREET

TWIZZLE
TAKES A RIDE

"Of course, not all of the stories are wrong," Missus Milliwhistle said thoughtfully. "The stories about gnomes are pretty much true. They live their lives deep underground, and they spend each day looking for gold and gems. Whenever a gnome finds something of value, he puts it in a secret hiding place. Each piece is hidden far from all of the others, so that a person who happened to find part of his treasure wouldn't know about the rest.

"Since gnomes are already below ground, it doesn't occur to them to 'bury' their treasure below their feet. Instead, they often hide it above their heads, sometimes just under the surface. As a result, people walking above ground often find the gnomes' treasure quite by accident. The gnomes constantly worry about their treasure, so they're never happy."

The Gnome

The grizzled Gnome within his keep
labors long 'neath mountain deep,
digging tunnels, mining jewels.
Most can see he's such a fool
to keep his treasure hid away
where it won't see the light of day.
By his own greed he is ensnared.
What good is treasure that's not shared?

"Did I tell you that just last week I saw a satyr right out here in the forest?" asked Missus Milliwhistle as she turned to the next picture in her book. "It is very unusual to actually see one, you know, because they're distrustful of people. But I sat quietly for a long time, and he didn't notice that I was even there.

"The Greek god of meadows and woodlands, and of shepherds and their flocks, was called Pan, who happened to be a satyr. Satyrs are half man and half goat. They live in the forest and love to play all of the time. Satyrs get along with almost every other creature because they never expect to get anything from anyone.

"Satyrs love stories and music, especially making up songs and then singing them. And their music is so beautiful. If you go deep into the forest and listen very, very closely, you can sometimes hear the melody of a satyr singing softly along with the breeze."

The Satyr

With tiny horns upon his head
the Satyr hears all that's said.
He won't oppose or disagree
with anyone's philosophy.
He'll listen 'till the story ends
and so he never lacks for friends.
And if the story's not too long,
it may become a satyr's song.

Missus Milliwhistle turned the page and gasped with pleasure. "Ah! Here's another forest creature that not many people are lucky enough to catch a glimpse of — the magical unicorn.

"Once there was a grumpy old man named Pliny who wrote that the unicorn was a ferocious beast with a single horn coming out of the middle of its head and feet like an elephant. It sounds to me like Mister Pliny happened across an altogether different creature and didn't bother to reason it out. He just assumed that because the beast in front of him had a single horn it must be a unicorn.

"If he had stopped to think he would have realized that a unicorn would never come anywhere near a grumpy old man. Unicorns are just too timid and shy. What would come close to a grumpy old man, of course, is a grumpy old rhinoceros."

The Unicorn

The gentle timid Unicorn,
with graceful, spiraled, golden horn,
once confidante to virgin maids,
safe from any manly raids,
lies sheltered in the forest deep,
a constant vigil his to keep.
And one that's honest, true, and fair
still may chance to glimpse him there.

Slowly turning another page in her big book, Missus Milliwhistle continued: "Legends say that the phoenix lives for a very long time, from 500 to 7,000 years. When this magical bird gets old — and I would say that 500 years is pretty old — it makes a fire in its nest, climbs in and burns itself up. Then it comes out of the fire as a brand-new young bird.

"Now, I don't know about the part where it builds a fire in its nest and climbs in. But I do know that the phoenix has a wonderful ability. Whenever it realizes that it is doing things that are not nice, or when it is unhappy, it imagines a fire in its mind and burns up all of its ideas about itself. Then it begins all over as the kind of bird it wants to be."

Then she looked right at Frog. "You could do the same thing, you know," she said.

"What's that?" asked Frog.

"Burn up the thought that we were having a story time without you. Then you could stop pouting," she said with a smile.

The Phoenix

The Phoenix, wondrous bird of fire,
who rises from the funeral pyre
with all the old self burned away,
begins his life anew this day.
He shows us all, if we can see,
to lose the past will set us free.
If we can break our old self's hold,
we can watch our dreams unfold.

"Speaking of doing things with your mind makes me think of Pegasus. Pegasus was a wonderful winged horse who brought joy and inspiration to all. He showed his bravery by carrying the hero Bellerophon to slay the deadly chimera. His beauty and sensitivity inspired even the muses, and it is the muses that inspire men and women to write poetry and songs, to paint and to make beautiful things.

"I like to imagine that my mind is like Pegasus, flying free, doing great deeds, visiting magical lands and bringing happiness to everyone I meet. So my little friends, from now on whenever you read a story, or someone tells you something, ride the Pegasus of your mind. Think for yourself, have the courage to do what you know is right, and always bring joy to others."

The Pegasus

Pegasus, a noble steed
of equine aviary breed,
mounts the sky on silvery wing,
a sense of wonder his to bring.
With starburst hoofbeats 'cross the sky,
the Angels cheer as he goes by.
And if you look inside, you'll find
a Pegasus within your mind.

Missus Milliwhistle carefully closed her book, taking care not to catch Frog's toes between its pages. "Tomorrow we will have a story time at ten o'clock, and you are all invited, especially you, Mister Frog," she said with a wink.

Dear Readers:

Did you find Olde Missus Milliwhistle, Buford Beetle, Elizabeth Lizard, and Frog, who was formerly known as Prince, in all of the pictures? Of course, they are not in the picture of the grumpy old man. Do you blame them?

ABOUT THE AUTHORS

Ron and **Val Lindahn** live deep in the woods of the North Georgia mountains with their son Sean, two cats, a dog, two birds, an occasional opossum, several dragons, and a number of other interesting beasties.

Val has worked as an illustrator for 25 years, bringing magic and a sense of wonder to life through her paintings in books, magazines, posters and movies. In addition to creating award-winning images, Val is an accomplished sculptor, cook and gardener, and is an expert in hairball analysis.

Ron has spent the past 48 years wearing his inner child out. Along the way he has worked as a professional photographer, filmmaker, ski instructor, jeweler, graphic designer, writer, yoga teacher, marketing consultant, illustrator, nail banger and mechanic, and he plays bass guitar with the Atomic Fireballs.

Val and Ron are judges for the international L. Ron Hubbard Illustrators of the Future contest.

Other books by Ron and Val Lindahn

The Secret Lives of Cats
How to Choose Your Dragon

To contact the Lindahns write care of:

Valhalla Studio
P.O. Box 24
Rabun Gap, Georgia 30568